HOW TO
DEAL
with GRIEF

Copyright © 2024 Stella Jack
All rights reserved.
ISBN 978-1-913455-62-0
No part of this book shall be reproduced or transmitted
in any form or by
any means, electronic or mechanical, including
photocopying, recording, or by any information retrieval
system without written permission of the author
and publisher.
Published by Scribblecity Publications.
Printed in Great Britain
Although every precaution has been taken in
the preparation of this book, the publisher and author
assume no responsibility for errors or omissions. Neither
is any liability assumed for damages resulting from the use
of this information contained herein.

Table of Contents

Introduction	5
My Story	9
Dangers of Grief	25
Tips to Conquer Grief	36
Conclusion	55

INTRODUCTION

Isaiah 61:1-3

1 "The Spirit of the Lord God is upon Me,
Because the Lord has anointed Me
To preach good tidings to the poor;
He has sent Me to heal the brokenhearted,
To proclaim liberty to the captives,
And the opening of the prison to those who are bound;
2 To proclaim the acceptable year of the Lord,
And the day of vengeance of our God;
To comfort all who mourn,
3 To console those who mourn in Zion,
To give them beauty for ashes,
The oil of joy for mourning,

> The garment of praise for the spirit of heaviness;
> That they may be called trees of righteousness,
> The planting of the Lord, that He may be glorified."

Recently, I had the privilege to encourage a dear one whose mother passed away about a month ago. She was battling with a lot of grief. As we talked, she was busy taking notes and writing the scriptures that I shared with her. Realising how much she wanted to record our conversation, I promised to email her the verses later in the day.

However, after I woke up the next morning, meditating and listening for the voice of the Holy Spirit, as has become my habit, I heard him tell me to write a book, putting down my journey handling loss and scriptures to help people struggling with loss.

I pray that as you read this book, your eyes will be opened to the power of the Holy Spirit and God's word in times of great loss or disappointment.

-1-
MY STORY

Growing up, I had an abnormal fear of death. I never wanted to hear about it, and I lived in constant fear of anything that had to do with death. To God be the glory, I was set free from this fear at 17 years old. However, I had seen people lose loved ones and grieve for loved ones, and the fear of losing a loved one bothered me. I remember vividly when my second cousin lost her husband in a ghastly car crash in Nigeria. When we went to visit her, her grief was so unbearable that she was sedated. This was also similar to a sister in my church whose husband also died unexpectedly. I am fortunate to have been born into a family with longevity; as a result, growing up, I never lost a close relative. I always wondered how I would cope should any member of my family die.

However, one day in January 2016, I remember studying **John 10:18**, which says,

> "No one takes it from me, but I lay it down of my own accord. I have authority to lay it down and authority to take it up again. This command I received from my Father."

This scripture was suddenly illuminated to me in a new way. Jesus was clearly saying that he was the one who laid down his life, and he had the authority to pick it back up again. I began to question the Holy Spirit because, when Jesus laid down his life, he was supposed to be dead. If he is dead, how does he pick it back up again? The Holy Spirit explained to me that when we breathe our last and transition to eternity, we are fully alive, and God can communicate with us. We can be given the option to come back or not. I came to understand that when believers die, they see eternity, and don't want to return. Little did I know at that time that my mother was going to pass away a couple of weeks later.

On February 7, 2016, I went to church with my family, and as it was our habit, we would stop over at my elder sister's house for lunch after church. That afternoon, as we arrived at her door, she handed me her phone, telling me that Mama had slipped into a coma. My twin brother was on the other end of the phone. He explained that our mom had laid down and calmly started to call on Jesus, and subsequently, she slipped into a coma. Shortly after, he said she stopped breathing. I asked him to call her back to life, but he refused, stating that on slipping into the coma, they had called and pleaded with her to come back, but she vehemently shook her head. He told me it was useless to pray for her to return because he knew she had decided it was time to transition into glory.

At that point, I had so much peace, remembering what the Holy Spirit had shown me concerning the power we have as children of God to lay down our lives or pick them back up. If only we all understood that the same authority Jesus had over his life we also have over ours. Many believers have their lives cut short because of ignorance. As the scripture says in **Hosea 4:6** and **Isaiah 5:13**,

> "My people are destroyed for lack of knowledge: because thou hast rejected knowledge..."

Satan is a master at taking advantage of our ignorance, and as a result, we can die prematurely if we don't exercise our God-given authority over death. Looking back, I remember my mother saying that, when she was ready, Jesus would take her home. She told a couple of people she would soon be departing this earth, and that was exactly how she passed. She lay down, and Jesus took her home peacefully. Hallelujah!!!

With my mother passing on that day, I had to deal with the emotions that followed. However, one thing was clear to me, and that was that my mom had chosen to depart this life. It wasn't forced on her by Satan or God. This understanding was from the revelation God gave me in John 10:18. I am grateful that God prepared me for this.

Different Types of Grief

Grief from Loss of a Loved One

Grief is a very powerful emotion that, if not checked, can ruin a person's life. The challenging thing about losing a loved one to death is that you can't control it. It can happen suddenly, out of the blue, as a result of numerous circumstances. Also, many people have had to grieve deeply as loved ones suffered over a long period and eventually succumbed to death. This can be very devasting if one is praying fervently for healing, but death takes place. In such situations, many people have had their faith shaken and wondered about God's goodness.

I pray that what I say next will not offend but be humbly received as gospel truth. It is critical to understand that loss does not determine the integrity of God. God remains faithful even when it seems like he has not come through. I say this because Jesus did all that was ever needed for our salvation, healing, and deliverance. When he hung on the cross, he said, "It is finished." The complete payment for our health was done, and it is up to men to appropriate health and healing for themselves. In the same way, it is up to man to accept or reject salvation from sin. God is not in heaven deciding who gets well and who dies. I pray you understand that because God is a good father, he wants us well and raised from the bed of affliction. Untimely death, by any means, does not give him glory or joy. However, regardless of how people die, the Holy Spirit is on hand to comfort us and give us peace.

Some people simply won't move on after someone passes because they live in regret. They blame themselves as they reflect on what they should have, could have, or would have done. Even if you didn't make the right choices, resulting in a person's death, I want to encourage you to lay your mistake at the foot of the cross and ask Jesus to cleanse you from all unrighteousness. Once you do that, receive his forgiveness, and above all, forgive yourself. If you refuse to forgive yourself, you make yourself more righteous than God, who considers you worthy of his forgiveness.

Grief from Loss of a Relationship

Another way people get hit with grief is through the loss of relationships. I am referring to dealing with the pain of breaking up with people who are still alive. Some examples are when there is a divorce, a breakup with a significant other or friends, the loss of a job, or a church hurt. Whatever the reason for these types of pain, God has healing available for us. In these cases, people feel rejected, and honestly, no one likes to be rejected or abandoned. Humans are social beings and were built for relationships. I have been through all these situations except for getting a divorce. To God be the glory, he brought me out of the horrible pain that came with all of them, and that is why I can say confidently that healing is available to you.

One of the reasons that rejection hurts so badly is that we have misunderstood human nature. We put people on a pedestal and forget that they are fallible humans like us. There's this erroneous idea out there that humans are inherently good. This goes completely against scripture. Check out these scriptures about men.

Jeremiah 17:9
"The heart is deceitful above all things, and desperately wicked: who can know it?"

Genesis 6:5
"Then the Lord saw that the wickedness of man was great in the earth, and that every intent[b] of the thoughts of his heart was only evil continually".

John 2:24-25
24 But Jesus did not commit himself to them, because he knew all men,
25 and had no need that anyone should testify of man, for He knew what was in man.

We hurt because we don't expect people to betray us. However, if we know that anybody is capable of falling into Satan's trap at a weak moment, then we won't be shocked by what our loved ones do to us. Think about it: you don't even trust yourself to make the right choices for you. That's why we shouldn't assume that others will.

My first betrayal happened in my college fellowship, where I was excommunicated along with three other believers because we were accused of holding some wrong doctrines. I have never forgotten the Wednesday mid-week service when our names were announced. I was so broken, weeping as I left the service, wondering what I had done wrong. Things got worse; many of my brethren in the major campus fellowships stopped associating with us because we were considered backsliders. I am so grateful to God that, although I was maligned and ostracised by some in the body of Christ, I never allowed it to affect my desire to continue in fellowship with believers.

For some who will read this book, you have allowed the church to keep you from fellowshipping with other believers. Let's consider Jesus and the betrayal he suffered from his disciples; he never allowed what they did to stop him from meeting with them. Jesus understood what man was capable of, and that was why he prayed on the cross that the Father would forgive those who hurt him because they didn't know what they were doing. Over and over, Jesus commands us to forgive and pray for those who despitefully use us. Here we see that when we pray for people who hurt us, we will save our hearts from negative emotions. The more you pray for your enemies, the more you will be healed. So, take a moment and pray now.

Another shift in mindset that will help you overcome a relationship loss is understanding that every relationship is for a time and a season. For example, although I went back to the leadership of the fellowship and made my case, pleading with them not to excommunicate me, they refused to reverse their decision. Even after they admitted their error, I wasn't allowed back. As I look back at what happened, I am grateful to God that I was forced out. As painful as it was at that time, God used it to launch me into revival, a great move of God that swept across many university campuses in Nigeria from 1984 to 1990.

A third thing that will help you during such times is knowing that when someone chooses to separate from you, it is likely because they no longer value you in their lives. Don't you ever grieve over people who don't value you or try to hold onto such relationships? When you understand the value God put in you, when people reject you, your mindset should be that of feeling sorry for them because they just missed out on someone of great value. See them as losers, not you. Yes, because if Jesus puts value on you, why should you sweat people?

Jesus was rejected by people he loved so that you can be accepted.

Isaiah 53:3
> He is despised and rejected by men,
> A Man of sorrows and acquainted with grief.
> And we hid, as it were, our faces from Him; He was despised, and we did not esteem Him.

I challenge you to let Jesus be enough for you. Another reason it hurts is because you make people idols by placing them ahead of your relationship with God. As a result, when they walk away, you slip into loneliness and self-hatred. You begin to wonder what you did wrong and blame yourself for a broken relationship. I once heard someone say, "25% of people you meet will never like you, no matter what you do. Another 25% may not like you initially but may change their opinion after some time. 25% will like you, but there are certain things you do that will make them stop liking you. However, there's the last 25% that will love you unconditionally regardless of what you do; therefore, focus your energy on building your relationship with them." I think that in life, you may not have up to 25% of people who will love you unconditionally. One thing is certain: Jesus will never stop loving you. Focus on building your relationship with him because he is enough for you. He is that friend who sticks closer than a brother.

If you are struggling with loneliness, it is because you truly don't know the abiding presence of the Holy Spirit. He is a real person, a bona fide companion sent to comfort and be with you.

John 14:16
> "And I will ask the Father, and he will give you another Helper, to be with you forever."

Let the Holy Spirit fill the vacuum left as a result of death or breakup. Yes, he can do that. I am not saying you should not miss people, but that you should not grieve unduly for them. Do not let your spirit be cast down; rather, let your heart be full of the joy that only God can give. This will differentiate us from people who don't have the Holy Spirit.

Finally, one of the signs of the last days is betrayal and rejection.
Luke 12:53
> "Father will be divided against son and son against father, mother against daughter and daughter against mother, mother-in-law against her daughter-in-law and daughter-in-law against her mother-in-law."

As the intensity of darkness increases, the separation between the children of God and Satan will continue. Unfortunately, this will cause divisions in families. Jesus told us that he didn't come to bring peace to the world, but a sword. Family members who don't believe the truth will turn against believers. We saw this in a demonstration during the COVID-19 pandemic, when people ostracised family members who refused to take the shots. We also had people cutting off relationships when someone decided to hold to the injunctions in scripture. We live at a time when people call good evil and evil good. Sadly, you may find yourself on a different side than members of your family. When you get rejected because of your faith, remember that Jesus was rejected. Rejoice and be exceedingly glad because you are counted worthy to suffer for Christ.

-2-
DANGERS OF GRIEF

God warned me about the dangers of grief/crushed spirit, and we will look at how grieving for an extended period can have very negative effects on our lives.

Grieving May Lead You to Doubt God's Love

When we let grief overwhelm us, it may open the door for Satan to sow seeds of doubt about the love of God. The enemy can start telling us that if God loves us, why did he allow the loss? This way of thinking suggests that God is responsible for what happened. Unfortunately, this was Job's mindset when he spoke in Job 1.

Job 1:21
> "And he said:
>
> "Naked I came from my mother's womb, And naked shall I return there. The Lord gave, and the Lord has taken away; Blessed be the name of the Lord.""

This verse has often been used to attribute death and loss to God. Nothing is farther from the truth because God isn't in the business of cutting short the lives of our loved ones. Satan is the one who comes to kill, steal, and destroy. Jesus came that we may have life and have it until it overflows. John 10:10. Do you realize that the only two people in scripture that God took while they were alive were Enoch and Elijah?

I appreciate the fact that many times we don't fully understand why someone died, especially if we prayed and stood in faith. That still doesn't mean God took them. No matter how much your loss doesn't make sense, never believe that God had a hand in it. Even though God has all power and authority, his ability to exercise them is limited by human participation. Man is still the god of this world.

To help you understand this, think about a landlord who owns a home but rents it to a tenant after signing a lease. The landlord has no legal right to enter his property without the tenant's permission. If he tries to, his tenant can call the cops on him for trespassing, even though the property belongs to him. Man gives God legal access to the earth through prayer, faith, and confession of the Word. Unfortunately, many people pray, but not in faith. As a result, when our prayer doesn't produce a result, we say, "But I prayed and God didn't answer."

Also, note that there's a limit to how much your faith can help someone else. A time comes when they need to agree with you.

You may be praying for someone to get healed while they are already thinking about their death. For example, my mom had made up her mind to depart and be with Jesus, so praying for her to live would have been useless. So, remember that God is good, and every good thing comes from him. God never gives us death and sickness. So, we should never allow grief to cause us to doubt God's love.

Sadness May Cause Serious Health Problems

Extreme sadness can create a variety of health issues, which may include depression, high blood pressure, insomnia, and a compromised immune system, to name a few. Grief can also be an open door for demonic oppression. Therefore, we must deal with negative emotions. Some people get so depressed that they lose their appetite or start to overeat. These abnormal eating patterns also bring along health challenges. Do not allow your enemy to use your loss as an excuse to afflict you.

Proverbs 17: 22
 "A merry heart does good, like medicine, But a broken spirit dries the bones."

This verse clearly shows that the state of our heart, which includes our mental state, is directly related to our physical health. Scientists have shown that being happy helps improve our physical well-being. This was one thing the Holy Spirit warned me about when my mother died. He made me understand that choosing to be happy was wisdom because I could avoid becoming sick.

I thank God that I have never had issues with my blood pressure. However, for those who battle high blood pressure, it is dangerous to allow grief to last for a prolonged period. Medical research indicates that a prolonged period of grieving can increase the possibility of developing blood clots and weaken the heart muscle so much that it causes *"Broken Heart Syndrome"*, also known as *Takotsubo Cardiomyopathy*.

In summary, grief can worsen health problems, affect the immune system as well as raise blood pressure.

We can see even science attests that we should be mindful of the state of our emotions, which is in line with God's word.

Proverbs 4:23
> "Keep thy heart with all diligence; for out of it are the issues of life."

Proverbs 18:14
> "The spirit of a man will sustain his infirmity; but a wounded spirit who can bear?"

Unfortunately, well-meaning people who have been influenced by human psychology encourage you to accept the "grieving process" rather than resist it by superimposing God's supernatural provision of comfort, joy, and peace, which comes from the Holy Spirit. This is why the Holy Spirit told me that each morning I must choose how I feel.

Choose to let joy in, especially as you have cried for more than one night.

Psalm 30:5
> "Weeping may endure for a night, but joy comes in the morning."

Isaiah 61:3
> "To appoint unto them that mourn in Zion, to give unto them beauty for ashes, the oil of joy for mourning, the garment of praise for the spirit of heaviness."

Another thing the Holy Spirit told me was that after people pass into glory, God isn't in heaven mourning, and neither are the ones who passed away because they are with him. This doesn't mean he sanctions or likes the circumstances under which they passed. He told me that being sad doesn't make him happy, and I needed to see things from his perspective. Yes, many die after extended periods of suffering, which hurts God's heart. This is because those people ought to have been healed, considering that Jesus paid the price for their healing. That notwithstanding, we shouldn't dwell on their suffering and have that imprinted in our minds so that we don't move beyond their pain. Knowing that yesterday is in the past, we should, like Paul, put it behind us and look into the glorious future that God has in store for us.

John 14:1-3

1 "Let not your heart be troubled; you believe in God, believe also in Me.
2 In My Father's house are many mansions; if it were not so, I would have told you. I go to prepare a place for you.
3 And if I go and prepare a place for

you, I will come again and receive you to Myself; that where I am, there you may be also.

A Friend's Experience

As I conclude this section of this book, I will share an experience I had with a dear friend whose mother recently passed away at 98.

We had been believing God that my friend's mom would overcome some health issues and move up to be with her in New York. However, some weeks later, she got the news that her mom had passed right after her 98th birthday. My friend kept asking me to keep her in my prayers. On my part, I did my best to encourage her with the same truths I shared here. I didn't fully grasp how badly she was handling her mom's passing until I went for the viewing. I noticed she was being helped to her feet by a family member who had a walking stick with her. When I asked her what was going on, she explained that her grief over her mom's passing had taken a toll on her body. When she stood, her legs wobbled. She had also lost any appetite for food. I was concerned for not just her but for her children, who recently lost their father. Their father's significant other did not let them know he had died and cremated his corpse immediately. So, for my friend to suddenly start experiencing such health challenges, it was a lot for her kids. One of her daughters was six months pregnant and didn't need to deal with the additional challenge of her mother's situation. Seeing all this, I immediately confronted my friend with the truths I share in this book. I rebuked her and challenged her to let faith arise in her because Satan was taking advantage of her.

As I did that, she humbly admitted that I was right and that she knew better than to wallow in grief. We prayed together, taking authority over the spirit of grief and depression. In faith, she asked me to walk with her to the coffin where her mother lay because she hadn't been able to do so without breaking down. She told me she needed to show Satan that his hold on her had been broken. Praise God! We walked to look at the corpse, and she was unassisted.

I kept reminding her that her mother died a believer and was at peace with Jesus. Also, if she continued on the path of grief, it would be counterproductive for her and her family, who needed her to be strong, not an emotional mess. I thank God she was humble enough to accept correction and didn't make excuses for how she had allowed Satan to get the upper hand in her situation by attacking her body. I want to reiterate that being joyful when we lose someone is not a sign that we don't love them, but an indication that we truly believe in the promise of being reunited with them shortly.

-2-
TIPS TO CONQUER GRIEF

These are ways that will help you overcome grief:

1. Take Charge of Your Emotions.

One thing I learned from Andrew Wommack is that how you react when you get a negative report goes a long way towards determining how you will handle the rest of the situation. The secret is that you must not fall apart like a $2.00 suitcase when you are hit with bad news. I thank God that I didn't fall apart emotionally when this happened. I harnessed my emotions as I processed the passing of my mother. I am grateful that, over the years, I have come to believe that the word of God is relevant in every situation. I was faced with the new challenge of losing my mom, who was a close friend and confidant. I moved forward knowing I could choose my emotions, which are subject to what I choose to think about.

The world's perspective on bereavement is that you grieve deeply and for a long time. Yes, that is what it ought to be for natural human beings who don't have the ministry of the Holy Spirit. Many times, I have had believers get defensive and argue with me or even take offence when I try to tell them that our case should be different. It is like they want to hold on to their pain and sorrow, which are eating them up. Psychology teaches us about the grieving process, but the word of God empowers us to circumvent this and be joyful in the face of loss. I am not trying to condemn anyone in this book, but to show God's provision in a difficult time.

The struggle many people have is how to overcome grief. Before you can overcome grief, you must first believe that it isn't God's will for you to wallow in it. There must be a holy dissatisfaction and rejection of grief in the same way we reject every negative thing thrown at us by Satan. There must be a clear understanding that God doesn't want us to experience the same type of grief as the rest of the world.

1 Thessalonians 4:13,
> " But I do not want you to be ignorant, brethren, concerning those who have fallen asleep, lest you sorrow as others who have no hope."

When we assimilate this glorious truth that we should not grieve like the rest of the world, then grief can be controlled by choosing to focus our thoughts on the fact that if you lose a loved one in Christ, you will see them again at the resurrection. While speaking with someone who lost her mom, she asked me,

"How do I control my thoughts?"
To control your thoughts, you have to first take responsibility for them. Thoughts are controllable. If you don't control them, they will run wild. They are like a moving car that is controlled by a steering wheel. Once you let it go, it will veer into dangerous territory. So, to control your thoughts,

• Talk out loud to yourself. Speak scripture-based words. For example,

> **Philippians 4:13,**
> "I can control my thoughts through Jesus Christ that strengthens me"
>
> **Colossians 3:2/ John 14:1-2**
> I refuse to allow my heart to be troubled because I believe in God and Jesus. There's a place in heaven for me and my loved ones.
>
> I set my mind on things above where Christ is. Where Christ is, there is

peace, joy and hope, so I have joy, peace and hope.

- Start to expose yourself to the type of information you want to fill yourself with. This can be in the form of Bible teachings, songs, and gospel messages that elevate your spirit. Also, avoid conversations with people who endorse the need for you to stay in the place of emotional pain and grief.

2. Allow the Holy Spirit to Comfort You

When we understand that scripture is divinely inspired, we will realise that there's no word in scripture void of power. Two of the Holy Spirit's names are Comforter and Helper. This means that he can comfort you when you need it and help you when you struggle with negative emotions and thoughts. This is very encouraging. Take a minute and soak this truth in. I remember the Holy Spirit speaking gently to me, "Allow me to comfort you because I do a pretty good job at it."

Isaiah 61:6b says that part of the Holy Spirit's ministry is "to comfort those who mourn."

John 14:26
>"But the Comforter, which is the Holy Ghost, whom the Father will send in my name, he shall teach you all things, and bring all things to your remembrance, whatsoever I have said unto you."

2 Corinthians 1:3-4
>**3** Blessed be God, even the Father of our Lord Jesus Christ, the Father of mercies, and the God of all comfort;
>**4** Who comforteth us in all our tribulation, that we may be able to comfort them which are in any trouble, by the comfort wherewith we ourselves are comforted of God.

All these verses affirm the powerful aspect of the ministry of the Holy Spirit which is to provide us with emotional comfort when we are hurting. The Holy Spirit constantly reminded me that receiving his comfort would be my choice. Each day, I intentionally received it by faith. I would use my words and say, "I receive the comfort of the Holy Spirit today." The same work of faith we practice in other areas must be done in this situation.

Another thing I learned to do was to put on the garment of praise instead of the spirit of heaviness.

Isaiah 61:3
> "To appoint unto them that mourn in Zion, to give unto them beauty for ashes, the oil of joy for mourning, the garment of praise for the spirit of heaviness."

Additionally, each morning when I woke up, I let joy in because weeping should only be for a night, and in the morning, joy was knocking at my door.

Psalm 30:5

> "...weeping may endure for a night, but joy cometh in the morning."

Based on these two scriptures, I visualized the spirit of joy knocking at the door of my heart to be let in. Also, I could see myself putting on a garment of praise after shedding off the spirit of heaviness. For the scripture to work, I had to take it literally. This is what Jesus meant in **Matthew 18: 3**,

> "And said, "Assuredly, I say to you, unless you are converted and become as little children, you will by no means enter the kingdom of heaven."

Children do not argue when you promise them something. They don't question your ability to deliver. Neither do they analyse or dissect the promise. They take your words at face value.

Another thing I did was to intentionally make myself rejoice. Sometimes, I put on praise music and would intentionally give God a sacrifice of praise by dancing to him. I vividly imagined my mother in God's presence and would think about how joyful she is. The more I thought about her joy, the happier I was. Several times, I reminded myself that even if Jesus asked my mom if she wanted to return to earth, her answer would be a resounding no. That being the case, if Mama is not sad where she is, why should I be miserable because she is gone? I made up my mind to see things from God's perspective, not the world's.

On the other hand, if you have lost someone whom you are not sure is in heaven, you are sad. My question to you is, "What difference does your grief make?" Can you, by being sad or weeping, bring the person out of hell? I encourage you to move on. Remember that every human has had the opportunity to accept or reject Jesus. Hopefully, while they were here, you spoke to them about Jesus, and they made their choice. Instead, use their demise as an opportunity to warn the living about eternity.

One misconception that causes people to be reluctant to let go of grief at the loss of a beloved one is that they feel guilty about being happy. Somehow, we are convinced that being sorrowful is evidence of how much we love the departed. We think that if we aren't crying a lot, it means we never really cared for the person. Honestly, anyone can shed crocodile tears when people die. In Jesus' time, there were professional mourners.

These people cried at the moment, and the next made fun of Jesus. If we are honest with ourselves, we will admit that grieving for the departed doesn't affect them in any way. It is something we do because we miss them and sometimes have regrets about what could have been. Like the adage, "Stop crying over spilled milk." The best thing you can do for someone is to love them when they are with you. Do not let anyone's opinion about you be the reason why you won't let the Holy Spirit comfort you.

Another misconception that gives people an excuse to be sorrowful is that even Jesus cried when Lazarus died. The issue is not that Jesus cried, but why he cried. Jesus did not cry because Lazarus died. Why would he cry because Lazarus died when he told his disciples that he was going to wake Lazarus up? Jesus intentionally let Lazarus die.

John 11:11-14

   11 These things He said, and after that He said to them, "Our friend Lazarus sleeps, but I go that I may wake him up."

   12 Then His disciples said, "Lord, if he sleeps he will get well."

   13 However, Jesus spoke of his death, but they thought that He was speaking about taking rest in sleep.

   14 Then Jesus said to them plainly, "Lazarus is dead.

   15 And I am glad for your sakes that I was not there, that you may believe. Nevertheless let us go to him."

Secondly, when he was speaking with Mary and Martha, he was trying to get them to understand that he had come to raise Lazarus from the dead right then, not at the resurrection. I believe Jesus wept because of their unbelief and inability to grasp what he was telling them.

> **John 11:23-25; 33-36**
>
> **23** Jesus said to her, "Your brother will rise again."
>
> **24** Martha answered, "I know he will rise again in the resurrection at the last day."
>
> **25** Jesus said to her, "I am the resurrection and the life. The one who believes in me will live, even though they die;
>
> **…33** When Jesus saw her weeping, and the Jews who had come along with her also weeping, he was deeply moved in spirit and troubled.
>
> **34** "Where have you laid him?" he asked.

"Come and see, Lord," they replied.

35 Jesus wept.

36 Then the Jews said, "See how he loved him!"

Note that the Jews assumed Jesus was weeping because Lazarus died. Jesus was troubled in spirit by their inability to grasp who he was. Additionally, there is no place where Jesus encourages people to be in grief over the loss of someone. even before his crucifixion. He cautioned his disciples about letting their hearts be troubled. He categorically told them not to allow their hearts to be troubled over what was about to happen. The secret to this was to put their faith in the Son and the Father while remembering that he was going to prepare a place for them.

John 14:1-3

1 "Let not your heart be troubled: ye believe in God, believe also in me.

2 In my Father's house are many mansions: if it were not so, I would have told you. I go to prepare a place for you.

3 And if I go and prepare a place for you, I will come again, and receive you unto myself; that where I am, there ye may be also.

My prayer is that you will remember that the death of a believer is not a finality but a temporary separation. Comprehend that Jesus, the Word of God, is able to comfort and heal you regardless of what you have lost.

3. Talk to God about it

Notice that I didn't say pray about it; this is because many people understand prayer as a monologue. Here, I am advocating for a conversation with God. Tell him that you are struggling, and listen to his comforting words and instructions on how to deal with your struggle. Also, because we are people of faith, it is important that we don't just turn it into a complaint; we bring along God's word.

For example:

"Father, right now I feel so much pain and heaviness, but I trust your word, which promises me joy. I thank you for being my comforter and my peace. I intentionally cast my cares upon you because you care for me. I refuse to be overwhelmed by sorrow because Jesus is my joy. Lord, I lean on you for strength because I have none. Thank you for renewing my strength."

4. Avoid Faithless People

Avoid conversations with people who will tell you that the pain of grief is okay. Tell them that's not what the word says. They will accept you or let you be.

5. Pray in Tongues

Using the amazing gift of praying in an unknown tongue, which is your heavenly prayer language, is key to overcoming grief. When we are faced with a painful loss, times come when we feel like we have no words to pray. We may not even feel like praying at all. Thank God, all these are feelings that are subject to change. Praying in tongues can change how we feel. It may not happen in five minutes or 10. Remember that life is a spiritual battle, and fighting grief is part of life. When you remember that peace and joy are promises from God, it is important to contend for them. Look at what the scripture says about the promises and hope we have in Christ.

Hebrews 6:18-20
18 "that by two immutable things, in which it is impossible for God to lie, we might have strong consolation, who have fled for refuge to lay hold of the hope set before us.
19 This hope we have as an anchor of the soul, both sure and steadfast, and which enters the Presence behind the veil,

20 where the forerunner has entered for us, even Jesus, having become High Priest forever according to the order of Melchizedek."

Because Jesus is the High Priest of our profession or confession, we know that as we battle in prayer to take hold of what the word promises, we are sure that God, who cannot lie, will do his part to ensure his joy and peace rule in our hearts. When you don't know how to pray, pray in tongues. Let your spirit man use your vocal cords to speak forth God's mysteries and promises. As you persevere in tongues, a time will come when you will experience a breakthrough.

1 Corinthians 14:2 and 4

2 For he who speaks in a tongue does not speak to men but to God, for no one understands him; however, in the spirit he speaks mysteries.

...4 He who speaks in a tongue edifies

himself, but he who prophesies edifies the church.

Edification means to build or encourage. So, this is a gift that, when you exercise, helps you. That is why you will feel the burden and pain lift from your shoulders as you persevere in tongues. Remember that grief and sorrow are all spirits, like joy and peace. So, stand your ground as you pray in tongues. Sometimes, you may have to do it several times a day until those negative spirits get the message that you won't allow them to hang on to you. They will eventually leave you permanently. Praise the Lord!

So, pray in tongues as much as possible. Pray until the burden and pain lift. If it comes back, pray! Pray! Pray! History and the Bible show us that Satan has been bitten several times, but he keeps coming back. The only way we can get away from spiritual battles is when we die. As long as you are on this side of eternity, remember that you will always be attacked by your adversary and his cohorts. Being under constant attack doesn't indicate you have a problem; rather, you are probably being a thorn in Satan's flesh. Just stand and fight the good fight of faith.

-4-
CONCLUSION

A few days ago, during my time with the Lord, he led me to the story of David and how he handled the death of his baby who was a product of his adulterous relationship with Bathsheba. This story shows how we should deal with grief in God's way.

2 Samuel 12: 16-23

16 David therefore besought God for the child; and David fasted, and went in, and lay all night upon the earth.

17 And the elders of his house arose, and went to him, to raise him up from the earth: but he would not, neither did he eat bread with them.

18 And it came to pass on the seventh day, that the child died. And the servants of David feared to tell him that the child was dead: for they said, Behold, while the child was yet alive, we spake unto him, and he would not hearken unto our voice: how will he then vex himself, if we tell him that the child is dead?

19 But when David saw that his servants whispered, David perceived that the child was dead: therefore David said unto his servants, Is the child dead? And they said, He is dead.

20 Then David arose from the earth, and washed, and anointed himself, and changed his apparel, and came into the house of the Lord, and worshipped: then he came to his own house; and when he required, they set bread before him, and he did eat.

21 Then said his servants unto him, What thing is this that thou hast done?

thou didst fast and weep for the child, while it was alive; but when the child was dead, thou didst rise and eat bread.

22 And he said, While the child was yet alive, I fasted and wept: for I said, Who can tell whether God will be gracious to me, that the child may live?

23 But now he is dead, wherefore should I fast? can I bring him back again? I shall go to him, but he shall not return to me.

Throughout this book, I have emphasised the need for Christians to have a different attitude about death. I feel persuaded to end this book with truths that the Holy Spirit recently revealed to me in the above portion of scripture.

David sinned against God by having an adulterous relationship with Bathsheba and eventually killing her husband, Uriah, to cover up the sin. The baby was a product of this terrible situation, and the consequence was the death of the child. Imagine that you are David. Imagine the shame and guilt he felt for being responsible for the mess. As we go through life, we will mess up, and this may result in the deaths of innocent people. Unfortunately, many people find it difficult to move beyond guilt. This is because the enemy beats us up to keep us down.

The first thing to learn from David is to take responsibility for your mistakes. Do not try to whitewash them or make excuses for them. Ensure that you are truly repentant, and deal with it before God. Humility and repentance will help our healing process. This also shuts up Satan, the accuser of the brethren. This is what David did in **2 Samuel 12** and **Psalm 51:4**.

> "Against you, you only, have I sinned
> and done what is evil in your sight;
> That You may be found just when You
> speak, And blameless when You judge.

David went before God, and after dealing with it, he knew that no one had a right to hold his sins against him. That was why he boldly pleaded for the life of his baby.

Secondly, know that God is good. Sometimes, you might not be responsible for a tragedy but may be trusting God to heal someone. Many times, we pray and exercise our faith, hoping that someone won't die, but yet they do. David did his best to save the life of his innocent child, but the child still died. That is heartbreaking and difficult to understand. My advice to you is that you shouldn't let what you don't understand come in the way of what you understand. One thing I believe we should all be assured of is that God is a good God who loves us unconditionally.

David knew these truths because, as a teenager, he had become intimate with God, so when he messed up, he did not walk away from his relationship with God. I encourage you to commit to knowing God for yourself through the study of his word and prayer. Stop depending on other people's prayers and prophetic words. There is always a time in life when there will be no one to hold your hand or encourage you; at such times, it's only your relationship with God that will pull you through.